DECORATIVE STAMPING

DECORATIVE STAMPING

Hundreds of Projects for Your Home

SASHA DOREY

PHOTOGRAPHS BY

Marie-Louise Avery

A Storey Publishing Book

STOREY

Storey Communications, Inc.
Schoolhouse Road
Pownal, Vermont 05261

THIS BOOK IS DEDICATED TO

WILLIAM AND BELLA

*The mission of Storey Communications is to serve our
customers by publishing practical information that encourages personal
independence in harmony with the environment.*

Published in the United States in 1995 by Storey Communications, Inc.
Schoolhouse Road, Pownal, Vermont 05261
Published in Great Britain in 1995 by Weidenfeld & Nicolson
Orion Publishing Group, Orion House,
5 Upper St. Martin's Lane, London WC2H 9EA

Library of Congress Cataloging-in-Publication Data

Dorey, Sasha, 1963-
      Decorative stamping / Sasha Dorey.
            p.   cm.
      "A Storey Publishing book."
      ISBN 0-88266-809-9
      1. Rubber stamp printing.   2. Interior decoration -- Amateurs'
manuals.   3. Paper work.   I. Title.
TT867.D67 1995
745.7--dc20   95-10532
                                                           CIP

ACKNOWLEDGMENTS
The author would like to thank Mary Baker, Becca and Bruno Charron,
Jon Dorey, Fancy and Blossom, Marion Field, Lorna and
David Haines, Matthew Hardy, Wendy Hopkins, Anna Macmiadhachain,
Dean Slavin, John and Emma Strange, Neil Thompson and Cathy Veale
for their help in the making of this book.

CONTENTS

✴

INTRODUCTION

Stamping is normally associated with rubber stamps, ink pads and paper, but that is really only the start of the story. Not only can you make yourself many designs of stamp from a humble potato or household sponge, you can also buy or have made sophisticated rubber stamps like those used by professional potters to decorate their ceramics. Furthermore, there are many wonderful ways of decorating with stamps. With an increasingly sophisticated array of paints available on the market, stamps can now be applied to virtually any surface from wood to ceramics, opening up a new range of decorative possibilities for the home.

The appeal of stamping lies in its simplicity. It is quick to do, original and inexpensive. A basic stamping kit of a stamp, paint and an applicator will enable you to decorate walls, fabric, furniture, make your own original wrapping paper and cards, jazz up old and tired tiles, or create a startlingly original quilt cover. As this book shows, the list is endless.

Interior decoration follows fashions just like any other industry involving style. However, although these fashions do not ebb and flow quite as rapidly as in the clothes industry, tastes and trends invariably change, leaving certain rooms looking quite dated. Stamping is a very inexpensive and effective method of bringing your rooms up-to-date, whether you choose a fashionable motif to stamp an entire room or simply pick out a few items of furniture to paint and stamp in different colours. Of course, if you tire of these colours and designs, you then won't resent changing them again as they took so little time, money and effort in creating. So, with the aid of this book, get yourself armed with a motif, roller and paint – and get stamping.

OPPOSITE: USE STAMPS ON ANY SURFACE TO ADD INTEREST

Materials and Techniques

Before tackling your first stamping project, read through this section as it shows you how to make and use stamps using different materials. There then follows specific information about each of the surfaces you can stamp on – fabric, wood, ceramics and paper.

OPPOSITE: THE BASIC MATERIALS FOR STAMPING ARE VERY FEW

HOW TO USE A MANUFACTURED STAMP

There are basically two methods of using a stamp; either with an ink pad or by applying paint. The second method is more versatile and economic, so this is the method used throughout the book unless otherwise stated. Ink pads certainly have their place in stamping, however; they are extremely quick and clean to use and so ideally suited for children to use. But as the pads are for ink alone, they can only be used with paper.

The simplest way of applying paint to a stamp is with a small roller. If this is not available, you can also use a small paintbrush, or even a piece of sponge. Of course, you don't necessarily need to put your paint onto a plate or paint tray, any other suitable dish would do such as the lid of a plastic container.

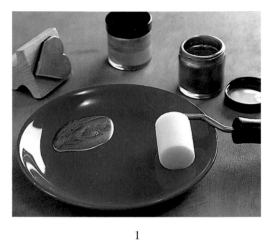

1

Pour out a small quantity of paint onto a plate or paint tray. If using paint in a tube, squeeze out a large blob and water it down with the thinner or water, depending on whether it is oil- or water-based.

YOU WILL NEED

Paint

—

Plate or paint tray

—

Roller

—

Stamp

2

Roll the paint onto and into the roller, rolling backwards and forwards over a clean part of the plate until the roller is saturated but not dripping with paint. There should be no blobs.

3

Move the roller across the stamp once or twice to ensure a full and even coverage. Then you can go ahead and stamp. You will probably find that you need to reapply paint after each print, but if you are looking for a more faded look, or an inconsistent finish, you could stamp two or even three times without adding more paint.

HOW TO MAKE A PAINT PAD

If you are unable to find a suitable roller or you prefer the idea of using an ink pad but find ink is not the suitable medium for your project, you could make up your own paint pad. This is an easy way of using paint but the coverage is not quite as smooth and even as it is when using a roller. You can use any water-based paint, including fabric paint and thicker paint in tubes, but this should first be watered down to allow for absorption into the sponge.

I have found that plastic baby wipe boxes are a good size for a paint pad and as they have built-in lids the pads won't dry out. Alternatively, use any plastic tub with a lid, such as a margarine container. The best type of sponge to use is one that isn't too dense, such as an ordinary household sponge.

1

Cut a piece of sponge to the right size so that it comfortably fits into your plastic container. Carefully wrap it with the piece of thin cotton and fit it snugly into the container.

YOU WILL NEED

Sponge

—

Scissors

—

Plastic container

—

Piece thin cotton

—

Paint

—

Metal spoon

—

Stamp

2

Pour the paint onto the pad (if you need to water down your paint, do this in a separate container) and then spread it around evenly with the back of the metal spoon until it is evenly absorbed.

3

Gently press the stamp onto the pad, repeating as frequently as is required.

HOW TO MAKE A POTATO STAMP

This must be the most commonly used and easy to make stamp – after all, most of us have a potato in our cupboard and a knife in our drawer. Obviously, the size of the design you wish to print dictates the size of potato you will need. Generally, the larger the potato the better, as this allows for any small mistakes.

For the first-time potato stamp maker, cut a very simple design, such as a heart or a diamond. Potatoes are very easy to cut, but until you have gained confidence do be careful as it is all too easy for the knife to slip.

A potato can easily be washed after each application so that another colour can be used. It can also be put in the refrigerator in a paper bag (not plastic as the potato will go soggy), for another day. It can then be stored in this way for up to five days.

YOU WILL NEED

*Tracing,
or parchment, paper*

—

Pencil

—

Thin cardboard

—

Scissors

—

*Potato
(the waxy variety)*

—

Sharp knife

—

Felt-tipped pen

—

Craft knife

—

Ink pad or paints

—

*Small roller
or paintbrush*

1

Trace a simple design or copy one from this book. Transfer this onto the thin cardboard (see page 90) and cut out to make your template. Next cut the potato in half using the sharp knife and hold the template firmly in place against one of the halves. Draw around the template with the felt-tipped pen.

2

Resting your hand on a table, hold the potato firmly and slowly cut around the design using the craft knife. Then carefully, piece by piece, cut out sections of waste to create a relief design.

3

If using an ink pad, simply press the stamp on the pad and then print onto your chosen surface. If using paints, use the small roller or paintbrush to apply paint to the potato (see page 10) and stamp away.

H O W   T O   M A K E   A   S P O N G E   S T A M P

Most of us have some kind of sponge in the house. Whether it be for the bath, make-up, cleaning the car or even the little round sponge that comes in the top of some vitamin tablet bottles. Some dish washing sponges have a scratchy backing for scouring pots and pans which acts very well as a built-in handle.

Foam rubber is also a good material to make stamps with although there are not so many household sources, but foam rubber sheeting is available from most craft shops and upholsterers. Polystyrene is another suitable material, as are erasers, although these are really only suitable for quite small motifs.

The texture of the sponge determines the depth of imprint. For example, a very open textured sponge will print a mottled image, whereas a cosmetic sponge will give a more solid image because it is denser. The photograph top right features several different kinds of sponge cut with either scissors or a craft knife.

To make stamps out of any of the above materials follow the instructions for making a potato stamp opposite or simply cut out the design using a sharp pair of scissors.

For more intricate shapes, it is easier to cut the designs out of felt than to gouge them out or incise them in other surfaces. Choose a design and draw or trace it onto paper. Cut it out and pin the design to a piece of felt. Then cut out the felt shape and simply stick it to a square of thick cardboard (or a cork for smaller designs) using PVA adhesive. This type of stamp can only be used with a single colour of paint as it is not washable.

S P O N G I N G

Sponging is a very pretty and decorative effect. It can be applied to both tiles and crockery as shown on page 21.

1
___
Using a loose natural or artificial sponge,
lightly stamp on a colour and leave it to dry.

2
___
Using a different sponge and a second colour,
stamp on top of the first colour.

3
___
When this is fully dried, use a foam or rubber
stamp of your choice to stamp on the pattern.

STAMPING ON WALLS

A wall painted with emulsion is the ideal surface on which to stamp. As the surface is matt and flat there is little possibility of the stamp sliding when you apply pressure. You can use any type of stamp, but those with a bit of give, such as a rubber or foam stamp, work best. Likewise, virtually any paint can be used to stamp with including emulsion, water colours, stamp paint, stencil paint and even oil paints.

Stamping onto a silk paint finish requires a little more concentration as the surface is slightly slippery. However, it is easier to correct any mistakes by using a damp cloth to wipe away the incorrect stamp. Gloss paint is not an ideal surface on which to stamp because the wet paint on the stamp is apt to slide about on the shiny surface. But with determination and a steady hand it can be mastered. To correct any mistakes, simply keep a damp cloth to hand and wipe away the error.

If you prefer a flawless finish, fill any holes and cracks with filler before stamping, but if you are happy with a more rustic style, the more holes and cracks the better. Although a bit of roughness and texture in a wall can add character, it's not possible to stamp onto a heavily textured wall such as woodchip or flocked paper. However, it is possible to stamp onto a papered wall, whether it be plain or printed. The end result is more refined than stamps on paint, but papering the walls merely to stamp onto them does entail considerably more effort.

Once you have decided on a colour scheme and stamp design, prepared your wall if necessary, and marked out a grid or border following the instructions opposite – you are ready to get going.

MARKING OUT

We all have our special ways of decorating. Some people like to thoroughly prepare, fill, sand and measure with spirit levels and plumb lines, while others are more haphazard and are happy to get on with absolutely no preparation using only their eyes to measure. The latter method is actually quite suited to stamping as a few flaws add to the character of the project. However, in many cases you will need to space your stamps regularly.

If you are not too concerned about having perfectly straight lines or do not own (or have no wish to own) a spirit level, a piece of string or ribbon will make a good substitute. Cut the piece of string to the desired spacing of the stamps and, starting from the top corner of the room, make a mark on the wall where you want the centre of your first stamp to be positioned. Hold one end of the string on this point and pull it taught, keeping it parallel with the ceiling. Make another mark at the other end. Continue to mark in this way, working horizontally along the top of the wall until you get to the end. Next, go back to the first mark and repeat vertically and then horizontally so that you eventually end up with evenly spaced rows of stamps.

To centre stamps on alternate rows as in the photograph to the right, cut a second piece of string so that it is exactly half the length of the first piece. Use it to mark the position of the first stamp on alternate rows.

STAMPING ON FABRIC

Fabric paints are now widely available in art and craft shops and some stationers. They come in a wide variety of colours including fluorescents, metallics and even glitters. As long as you use the same make of paint, it is possible to mix the colours to exactly the shade you want. Some of these paints require fixing with heat (ironing on the reverse of the fabric once the paint is dry), while others simply set as they dry. Full instructions are always supplied with the paint.

It is advisable to use a hard stamp on fabric (ideally a manufactured one), as you need to press quite hard to ensure full and even coverage. Foam and sponge stamps are not recommended.

For the best results, choose finely woven fabrics with little or no texture as the closer the weave the better the print. Stamping is especially effective on glazed cottons, silk and plain sheeting. This last is very cheap and ideal for making bedlinen as it can be bought in wide widths. If you stamp onto a heavily textured fabric you may find that the print is incomplete and needs filling by hand.

Before printing, iron the fabric and spread it over a clean, flat and hard surface. If you are working on a small piece of fabric you may want to keep it in place with strips of masking tape. Unfortunately, mistakes cannot be corrected so it is wise to practise on an off-cut of the same fabric beforehand.

Marking out is done in the same way as for walls (see previous page) using dressmaker's chalk which can be brushed off. But as the areas covered when stamping on fabric are generally small it is not always necessary to mark out, especially if you feel confident enough to stamp by eye.

OPPOSITE AND ABOVE: FABRIC PAINTS ARE AVAILABLE IN A WIDE VARIETY OF COLOURS AND ARE BEST USED ON FABRICS WITH LITTLE OR NO TEXTURE

STAMPING ON WOOD

Styles in interior design change in the same way as clothes styles, though thankfully not as rapidly, and with a coat of paint in a fashionable colour and a little decoration, furniture and accessories can be effortlessly brought up-to-date. And if and when you tire of this colour and design, simply paint it again.

Most pieces of wood are, in fact, painted surfaces as it tends to be the paint finish you are stamping onto and not the wood. As with walls (see page 14), it is possible to stamp onto any painted surface although a glossy surface requires a steady hand to ensure the painted stamp does not slip. You can use stamp paints, acrylics and oil-based paints to stamp on furniture. If you require a durable finish then you should varnish over the stamps with a matt polyurethane. Stamping onto wooden floors, for example, is a very effective decoration. You can either paint the floor and then stamp, as shown on page 75, or stamp directly onto bare or varnished wood. To ensure their durability, paint a coat or two of varnish over the stamps.

You can also stamp onto bare, untreated wood very successfully as the paint acts almost like a stain and is quickly absorbed into the wood. Any type of paint will work well, but mistakes cannot be simply wiped off. Instead, after removing as much paint as possible, you will then need to sand off any residues. If you are stamping a piece of furniture that will receive a lot of wear and tear, such as a chair, it is well worth painting on a few coats of varnish to protect the decoration.

If a piece of furniture has been waxed to protect the wood, remove it before stamping by rubbing white spirit over the wax and then sanding with a fine grade of sandpaper. Similarly, if you have a battered piece of furniture to decorate and you want to make it smoother, apply an all-purpose wood filler over any gashes and when it is dry, sand it smooth.

OPPOSITE: YOU CAN STAMP ON ANY WOOD, WHETHER IT IS PAINTED OR BARE

STAMPING ON CERAMICS

Few of us own our own kilns or even have access to them so the wider availability of cold, or low temperature ceramic paints has opened up a whole new craft. Cold ceramic paints are those that need no heat treatment to set. Once dried they are washable, although not in a dishwasher. For a more resilient finish, use ceramic paints that need to be fired in a domestic oven at a temperature of about 180°C (350°F, gas mark 4) for 10 minutes or according to the manufacturer's instructions. These paints can be used on any glazed ceramics (but they are not suitable for any items that may come into contact with your mouth), and are available in art and craft shops.

Sponge and foam stamps are ideal for use on ceramics as they will not slide about on glazed surfaces and their softness facilitates stamping on a curve (see page 63). The density of the sponge or foam dictates the quality of the print so for a solid print you need to use a denser type of foam stamp (see page 13).

Stamping onto tiles which are already fixed to a wall and so cannot be baked has to be done with cold ceramic paint. If your tiles are already plain and you simply want to stamp a pattern onto them, then just stamp straight onto the tile. Cold ceramic paints are solvent-based so any mistakes can be wiped off the tile using the appropriate manufacturer's cleaner. The same applies to cleaning the stamp and applicator and, for this reason, a small paintbrush is a better applicator than a sponge roller as this will happily absorb a whole pot of cleaner in one go.

 If you want to totally transform existing patterned tiles then you first need to paint them. To date, specific tile paint is not available, but concrete floor paint is extremely tough and durable and can be painted directly onto glazed tiles. Allow to dry and then stamp.

OPPOSITE: CERAMIC PAINT SHOULD BE USED FOR DECORATION ONLY; IT SHOULDN'T COME INTO CONTACT WITH YOUR MOUTH

21

STAMPING ON PAPER

Paper is the most straightforward surface onto which to stamp because you can use any type of paint or ink; any type of stamp, and – indeed – any type of paper, as you will see in the following chapter. There are so many beautiful and interesting types of paper and paper products available today, all of which can be roughly torn and layered and stamped, that it is possible to make all sorts of fabulous cards and stationery items. Choose from textured, handmade papers, sugar paper (available from craft shops and confectioners), tissue paper and crepe paper, each of which have their own particular qualities.

Papier mâché is now a very fashionable craft and a perfect medium to stamp onto. Or you can buy sophisticated ready-made papier mâché blanks such as trays, clocks, wastepaper tins and hat boxes (see page 96) which are just calling out to be stamped!

OPPOSITE: PAPER IS THE MOST FREQUENTLY USED SURFACE ON WHICH TO STAMP – AND THE MOST STRAIGHTFORWARD

EMBOSSING

For that extra special occasion, embossing will embellish any card, tag, invitation or announcement. Here is how you do it.

YOU WILL NEED

Embossing ink

—

Embossing pad

—

Stamp

—

Embossing powder

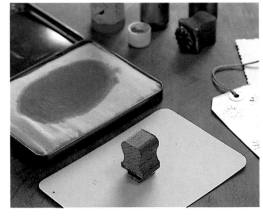

1

Apply the embossing ink to the surface of a dry pad and massage it into the pad using the spout of the ink bottle until the ink is absorbed. Stamp a wet image onto your object using the embossing ink.

2

Quickly sprinkle embossing powder over the ink and tap off any excess powder. Finally, hold the powdered image over a heat source such as an iron or toaster and the powder will melt to produce a glossy, raised finish.

Stamping on Stationery and Paper

Perhaps the most frequently used surface for stamping onto is paper, and with this in mind here are numerous ideas for ways in which to use stamps. Ranging from stationery items such as greetings cards, writing paper and invitations to other paper products such as photograph frames, wrapping paper and gift boxes, there is no shortage of ways in which to use your stamps. Here there are also ways to decorate table settings with paper stamped items: how about decorating crackers, napkins and hats with gold-stamped motifs for Christmas, or adding to the jollities of a children's party with brightly stamped tablecloth, cups and plates?

GREETINGS CARDS

The special quality of handmade cards and stationery lie in their originality and by using today's wonderful recycled and textured papers and a simple stamp, making them can be as much fun as receiving them. For example, by layering two or more torn-edged papers and stamping a golden heart in the centre you create an instant – and stylish – Valentine card. Similarly, by using other designs such as elephants and stars you can make unique and wonderful greeting cards for all occasions.

Sending letters and notes is even more pleasurable when you have designed your own paper and envelopes, either by using a single stamp or a border. Children can have a lot of fun making their own stamps and using them to create a letterhead on those birthday thank-you letters. Animal designs are always jolly and well liked and can be used by both children and adults. Simpler shapes can be cut out of foam or potatoes (see pages 12-13), but there is such a vast choice of stationery stamps available on the market today it would be a shame not to have one or two in your cupboard.

OPPOSITE: THE TEMPLATE FOR THE HEART IS ON PAGE 91

WRAPPING PAPER, GIFT BOXES AND BAGS

Gift wrapping is becoming increasingly sophisticated and glamorous, fun and adventurous. We would all love to own a drawer full to the brim with lovely wrappings for each occasion but most of us are not that organized. Besides, buying a whole year's worth of wrapping papers and boxes would cost a fortune.

A realistic alternative is to have a drawer full of inexpensive tissue paper and a stamp kit – or just a potato. You don't even need to use tissue paper, why not stamp gold onto newspaper? For the quickest wrapping paper ever, try stamping old newspaper, brown paper or even comic paper with a wine cork and whatever colour paint you have to hand. You could even paint string to bind it. And for a truly spectacular result, finish your present with a layer of cellophane. Don't throw away those brown and white paper food bags; instead, keep them and stamp them with gold or silver to create fabulous gift bags. There really are many ways to create beautiful gift wraps from boring household items – so start now.

ABOVE: THE TEMPLATE FOR THE HEART IS ON PAGE 91, AND THE DAISY IS ON PAGE 93

OPPOSITE: THE TEMPLATE FOR THE PETALS IS ON PAGE 95

INVITATION AND ANNOUNCEMENT CARDS

Some of us find smart invitations either rather dull or somewhat expensive. Handmade cards can often look a bit too handmade for certain occasions, but by using stamps and either gold or silver paint or embossing powders (see page 22) you can achieve a professional but still unique result.

For this kind of project you will need to use quite tiny stamps that could be too difficult to make. But if you have a specific motif or border pattern in mind it is possible to have it made up by a rubber stamp company or at a stationers. You could even have the entire invitation, including words and border, made up into one large stamp. The same could be done for birth announcements, menu cards and change of address. You might even find that one simple At Home card with your name, address and telephone number could serve for numerous occasions, saving the bother of having cards made up again and again.

You need not stick to repeating motifs along the top and bottom, or completely around the edge of the cards. Among the cards featured in the photograph opposite there are single stamps simply positioned in the middle of cards and a more abstract design placed at the top - notice how these last have been stamped so that the left side of the card is a mirror image of the right.

OPPOSITE: THE TEMPLATE FOR THE DAISY IS ON PAGE 93

PICTURE FRAMES

Photographs of family and friends which evoke very special memories warrant a beautiful frame, as do some greetings cards either because they are attractive or because they were sent from someone important. Or why not make up your own picture using the techniques shown on pages 26-7 and then frame it in a pretty and original mount? It does not cost very much to have a mount made up by a picture framer and some framers even keep a box of off-cuts which they will happily sell at a reduced price. Alternatively, you could cut your own mount out of thick cardboard, using a set square and sharp craft knife, and then decorate it with some simple stamps using the ideas outlined below.

Choosing suitable stamps and colours depends on the style and colour of your picture or photograph. For a more formal photograph such as a wedding or christening, you might choose a grand motif such as a fleur de lys or star, and stamp it using gold or silver paint, or silver ink if you are using mounting board.

For a more relaxed photograph of children, why not use a small circle stamp, as shown here? This was stamped using a wine cork and gold paint. What could be simpler? For variety, a diamond stamp cut from foam rubber was stamped on a frame before adding the circles over the top. The combination of these two simple stamps looks stunningly effective.

Cascades of ivy make a very pretty border and the design shown in the photograph opposite is suitable for any kind of picture. This particular stamp was made by cutting the design out of thick felt and sticking it onto a cork (see page 13).

OPPOSITE: THE TEMPLATE FOR THE GOLD STAR IS ON PAGE 90

A CHRISTMAS TABLE

Stamps really come into their own at Christmas. In the photograph opposite, they have been used for table decorations but they are, of course, equally perfect for wrapping paper, Christmas cards, gift tags and even for adorning fabric stockings.

Designs such as holly leaves and berries, Christmas trees, cherubs and stars can transform a plain paper tablecloth and napkins into a dazzling Christmas setting for all the family. You can even make your own Christmas crackers using toilet rolls and stamped tissue paper, filling them first with little gifts and stamped hats and, of course, the all-important snap. Before stamping a tablecloth, decide whether it is worth decorating a fabric cloth which can be used year after year or a disposable paper cloth which can be thrown away at the end of the meal. If your tastes change with the trends it is probably best to choose the second option and then every year you can stamp a different theme. Your choice will obviously dictate the type of paint or ink you can use with the stamp.

It is then time to decide upon a theme and the pattern. A delicate border of golden cherubs would look very tasteful and reserved as would a liberal scattering of green holly leaves. You could paint in the berries by hand, as has been done in this picture. Napkins can be stamped to match the tablecloth, as could placemats, place names and menus: it just depends on the extravagance of your Christmas dinner. Other Christmas ideas include stamping a wrapping to cover the Christmas tree tub; making decorations by cutting out a stamped image in card and threading it onto the tree, or stamping a border onto paper and cutting it out to make a garland.

OPPOSITE: THE TEMPLATE FOR THE STAR IS ON PAGE 90, AND THE HOLLY LEAF IS ON PAGE 93

A CHILDREN'S PARTY

Add to the excitement of a child's birthday by letting the birthday girl or boy decorate their own party table! All you need is a paper tablecloth, plain paper cups, plates and napkins, non-toxic paints, a paintbrush and a stamp of some description. A simple round potato stamp as shown here is very effective when used with several colours. Stamp several times using one colour first, clean the potato with a damp cloth, then stamp several more circles with the next colour, and so on.

The best way to apply paint onto the stamp in this instance is with a paintbrush as it is the easiest and quickest applicator to wash out. As you are applying several different colours, you will be doing a lot of washing out, so why not make life as straightforward as possible. Always use non-toxic, water-based children's paints and avoid stamping around the rim of the cups and the centre of the plates.

Of course, you can design a more specific theme suited especially to your child. Favourites such as tractors, dinosaurs, cartoon characters, teddies and even beetles are all readily available as commercial stamps. You might choose to stamp creatures all around the edge of the tablecloth and perhaps just one each on the napkins, or perhaps you might prefer to go for groups of animals scattered right across the table. You could also stamp up pretty little party bags, party hats, cake surrounds, and why not treat the children to homemade birthday crackers? These are made in the same way as Christmas crackers using a toilet roll and some stamped tissue paper (see the previous page).

OPPOSITE: CIRCLES CAN BE STAMPED
USING EVERYDAY OBJECTS SUCH AS A CORK

A WEDDING TABLE

Whether as an exercise in saving money or just a desire for a uniquely magical wedding, stamping can certainly play its role in all sorts of ways. Starting with the invitations, adorn them with borders of golden initials, hearts or stars, or have a stamp made up by a rubber stamp company of the entire invitation, including all the wording. Stamp it onto thin cardboard, or onto a deckle-edged textured paper which is then stuck onto thin cardboard. The invitation would look both stunning and very unusual, especially if envelopes are stamped to match.

Set the tables for a magical celebration using your own, unique table linen, menu cards and place names. Some paper tablecloths now look just as good as fabric ones as they are thick, soft and luxuriant. Enriched with some golden initials (the bride's and groom's, naturally), little hearts or stars, they would look quite amazing. And for an even more ornate table, stamp your chosen motifs onto squares of muslin with gold or white and layer them on top of either paper or fabric tablecloths. Stamp paper or muslin napkins to complement the tablecloths and as a final touch decorate menu cards and place names in the same theme. If you dare to be different, how about stamping the wedding dress fabric or at least the groom's waistcoat and page boys' bow ties?

Gold is usually the first choice for wedding decorations, but pastel shades can be just as successful, as can white on white. Tiny white star stamps on white fabric would look very delicate and pretty, and be subtle too as it would be mainly the textural contrasts that come through.

OPPOSITE: THE TEMPLATE FOR THE HEART IS ON PAGE 91

DECORATING BOOKS

Blank notebooks can be used for all manner of things, ranging from cookery books and address books, to diaries or sketchpads. Covering shop-bought books with stamped paper, and perhaps tying them with pretty ribbons to keep inquisitive readers at bay, makes them that little bit more personal, less mundane.

Choose from among the many textured papers available, as in the photograph opposite, or perhaps go for simple brown paper, layers of tissue paper, or plain wrapping papers, and stamp onto them the motifs of your choice. The simple stars used here work well as a striking abstract design, but you might choose to link in the stamps with the subject content of the book. Flowers for a gardening diary, hearts for musings on loved ones, simple house outlines for an address book.

To cover a book, open it out flat and cut around the paper allowing 2.5cm (1in) borders around the edge to fold around the cover. Snip the corners so that they mitre neatly around the edges, and cut to the edge of the book on either side of the spine. This then leaves you with a small tongue which can be tucked into the spine at top and bottom. To make sure that the cover stays in place, spray a light coating of spray adhesive onto the wrong side of the paper and then smooth it gently in place. For further protection, consider covering the stamped paper with a piece of clear self-adhesive plastic. This would be especially useful for a book that is going to be carried around alot, such as a travelog.

If it is important that your stamped design is centred to the book – or that it should be vertical – cut the paper before stamping so that you can prepare some exact measurements and guidelines.

OPPOSITE: THE TEMPLATE FOR THE STAR IS ON PAGE 90

Living Rooms

Stamping a heraldic or celestial design onto a rich colour immediately evokes a sense of opulence. Any living room can be transformed in a matter of hours with a little imagination, a stamp or two and a pot of gold paint.

Designs such as fleurs de lys, stars and coronets are always very popular in living rooms and are attractive and very easy to use either as a border or to cover an entire wall or curtains. The walls in this picture have been painted in a rich green emulsion, but a similar effect could be achieved using a deep blue, red or even an ecclesiastical purple. Or for quite a different feel, see the alternative colourway on pages 48-9.

SOFT FURNISHINGS

If you want a bold print, it is important to use a fabric with little or no texture. Silk is a wonderful fabric to stamp onto and it really warrants that extra embellishment of gold. But it is expensive and so is usually used for smaller items such as cushion covers and lampshades (see overleaf). Artificial alternatives include acetate. This fabric doesn't feel quite the same but the same look is created. Likewise, the curtain material in the photographs on the previous page and below is a medium-weight Indian cotton on which fabric paint works well.

If you plan to sew your own cushion covers it is a good idea to stamp onto the unsewn fabric so that if you do make a mistake you haven't wasted time or fabric cutting it out. Simply move along the fabric a bit and start again. As cushions are small, it is usually sufficient to stamp by eye, but if you do want precise spacing, mark out your pattern using dressmaker's chalk which can be brushed off. Grid patterns and borders using single or combined designs are equally effective.

ABOVE: THE TEMPLATE FOR THE STAR IS ON PAGE 94, AND THE FLEUR DE LYS IS ON PAGE 95

OPPOSITE: THE TEMPLATE FOR THE STAR IS ON PAGE 92, AND THE CROWN IS ON PAGE 94

LAMPSHADES

Although fiddly, it is possible to stamp onto a ready-made lampshade. The problem lies not so much in the curve of the shade as in the difficulty of applying pressure when stamping. The best technique is to lie the shade across an opened, flat hand and then stamp onto the shade using the opened hand as a backing.

There is, however, a wonderfully simple alternative: use a lampshade kit which comprises a frame and most importantly a flat, sticky-backed shade onto which you can glue any fabric or paper of your choice. This enables you to do your stamping before sticking the material onto the flat shade. A big advantage of this is that if you should happen to make any mistakes, you can start again on another piece of fabric before sticking it in place. The shade is then curved, glued and attached to the frame to create a unique lampshade designed to fit your exact taste. Lampshade kits are supplied with full instructions and are available from craft shops or by mail order (see suppliers on page 96).

ABOVE: THE TEMPLATE FOR THE PAISLEY MOTIF IS ON PAGE 91

OPPOSITE: THE TEMPLATE FOR THE CROWN IS ON PAGE 94

CHANGING COLOURS

To create a more contemporary, though still classic, look like the room in the photograph opposite, use abstract designs and soft colours. These walls have been decorated with a pale yellowy-brown emulsion paint and then when dry wiped over with a watered-down white emulsion paint with a soft, damp cloth. The end result is a wonderful soft, chalky appearance. It has then been stamped with an abstract design copied from an old Iranian tile in a well-spaced grid pattern (see page 15). This somewhat exotic look is continued using palm tree designs on the curtains and paisley and pineapples on the cushions.

The curtains are made of calico which has a good texture for stamping onto. Enhanced with gold, they look very rich and sumptuous, toning in beautifully with the painted walls. Again like the walls, the curtains have been stamped in a simple grid pattern using only one design – but a different one, for a touch of variety. They would look equally as attractive if a smaller stamp of a complementary design was dotted in between.

The palm tree motif has also been used on the cushions, together with the wall stamp and an additional design – the traditional paisley. Paisley shapes are extremely versatile and look stunning in virtually any situation and in any colour. Here, they are not only stamped in gold like the rest of the motifs in the living room, but also in white onto one of the cushions for some subtle variety. For a truly oriental look, why not stamp a dark earth-coloured paisley onto a rich red wall or fabric? You could even add small dots of gold for extra depth – you would have to do this by hand, of course.

OPPOSITE: THE TEMPLATES FOR THE PAISLEY MOTIF AND PALM TREE ARE ON PAGE 91

THREE

Dining Rooms

Dining rooms as such are becoming less common today as more and more people tend to make their kitchen a family room. If the latter is the case, then the design and colour theme must be one with which you feel comfortable as a lot of time is spent in this room. Softer, washed-out tones are likely to be the most suitable.

To avoid a cluttered visual impact, a delicate border of white fish rather than a grid pattern has been stamped on the wall in this dining room. Using light colours to stamp with ensures that the decoration is diffused and not too dominant and paintings and objects d'art can then be hung alongside most successfully.

Alternatively, if you have a formal dining room which is not used on a regular basis, consider using much stronger colours and themes similar to those shown on pages 42-7. Sumptuous colours and baronial motifs provide a perfect backdrop to feasting.

TABLECLOTH AND NAPKINS

Attractive table linen, curtain fabrics, cushion covers and bedlinens generally command rather unattractive prices. But with the aid of a stamp or two, some fabric paint and inexpensive fabrics such as calico, plain cottons and muslin, it is possible to effortlessly create your own sumptuous designs, tailormade for each setting. For example, a constellation of stars on floaty muslin drapes look both romantic and luxurious, while several multi-coloured stamps on a plain white quilt cover will jazz up any child's bedroom.

Here, to give an impression of freshness, a light green, blue and yellow have been sponged onto the tablecloth (see page 13) with an open-grained sponge and then stamped with gold fruit. These are always a favourite design in the dining room, whether used as here in a light fashion or stamped onto darker, bolder colours to create a more luxurious quality. Simple fruits like these could easily be cut out of sponge.

Stamping a tablecloth is an ideal way to get a new lease of life out of something that no longer suits your colour scheme or you are simply bored with. If you do not have an old tablecloth to hand, then why not make one out of inexpensive sheeting? A muslin tablecloth can look absolutely stunning with tiny stars, shells or hearts. Napkins can either be decorated in exactly the same way or to complement the tablecloth.

Today, fabric paints are not only readily available but also very versatile. Some stamp paints can be used on both walls and fabric with no need for heat sealing, enabling you to use the same shade on all surfaces. Table linen decorated with fabric paint is fully machine washable but you should follow the instructions given for the particular paint used.

OPPOSITE: THE TEMPLATE FOR THE GRAPES IS ON PAGE 93

DECORATIVE DETAILS

Painting furniture is quick and easy and so gives a wonderful sense of satisfaction. For today's washed and distressed look, there is no need to remove any existing paint as the more layers of paint the better. Simply sand lightly to roughen the surface so that the paint will adhere and then paint on a white undercoat, not worrying how even it looks as it will be covered by subsequent layers. Allow the paint to dry completely and then apply a second coat of your chosen finished colour. Rub the whole piece with furniture wax and then use wire wool to selectively rub away areas of paint to reveal the colours underneath. The article is now primed for stamping.

The size and shape of the piece of furniture will dictate what type of pattern you use. As the walls in this dining room are sparsely decorated, the wooden serving tray and the front of the dresser have been thoroughly stamped using the same fish design, as have the curtains behind.

RIGHT AND OPPOSITE:
THE TEMPLATE FOR THE FISH IS ON PAGE 94

FOUR

Kitchens

There are a multitude of surfaces and utensils that can be stamped in the kitchen as well as more decorative objects such as terracotta pots and bowls, dishes and plates. Instinctively, it is tempting to decorate with foodie motifs such as fruit, fish and vegetables. But why not decorate with your favourite design and colours? After all, most of us spend a lot of time in the kitchen.

For a truly rustic and somewhat al fresco look, a plaster paint effect dotted with a few hearts is both welcoming and homely. To achieve the paint effect, first paint the wall with butter yellow emulsion. There is no need to prepare the surface as imperfections and bashes add to the aged effect. Next, apply a coat of watered-down terracotta pink emulsion using an old damp cloth, or for a more even effect, a paintbrush. The hearts can then be applied either at random or in a more formal grid pattern (see page 15), as featured in the photograph to the left.

PLATES AND POTS

These attractive plates and terracotta pots have been decorated using the sponging technique shown on page 13 and simple sponge stamps and ceramic paints. The plates were first sponged with two different colours and then when the paint was dry they were stamped with colours and designs to complement the walls. The daisy on the left-hand plate is made up of two stamps – a simple round and an oval petal shape – and the pansy on the right is similarly made of two stamps – circles and hearts. The plates were then put in an oven at 180°C (350°F, Gas mark 4) for 10 minutes to set the paint. Following paint manufacturer's instructions, these plates are suitable for decorative use only and should be washed by hand.

Terracotta pots make great containers for holding miscellaneous objects and they are easily decorated with small, simple stamps, although you need to hold the pot steady as you carefully stamp around the curve. The pots featured in the photograph here have been stamped with a combination of small stamps, some along the rim and others around the main body of the pot. As terracotta pots tend not to conform in shape and texture it is fun to emphasize this by altering the patterns slightly from pot to pot. Try different paint colours too – pastel shades contrast subtly with the terracotta background. You can use either cold ceramic or emulsion paints.

Should you decide to use these plant pots for what they were originally intended, you might decide to stamp a simplified version of what is growing inside it. A daisy, for example, is easily done (see above), or herb leaves would look great. If cleaning the pots, the stamps won't survive too much scrubbing, but then this can be to your advantage because you won't necessarily always want to be growing the same things.

OPPOSITE: THE TEMPLATE FOR THE HEART IS ON PAGE 91, AND THE DAISY IS ON PAGE 93

CHANGING THE COLOUR SCHEME

Over the past few years a new room in the house has evolved – the family room. Basically, this is the heart of the house, a kitchen with an added living or play area. Such rooms require a style that will appear to the whole family. Black and white always look sophisticated but in using stamps such as animals the whole tone is softened and made more appealing to the younger members of the family. Black and white have the added bonus of mixing happily with virtually any other colour so that visible tins, jars and bottles all look quite colour coordinated and do not clash. Initially these tiles were blue and white but now they have been painted with concrete paint for a more uniform feel and stamped with cold ceramic paint.

Plain blinds can be bought in kit form and cut to fit any size window. Here they have been most effectively stamped with fabric paint, continuing the cow motif across the window.

ABOVE AND OPPOSITE: THE TEMPLATE FOR THE HEART IS ON PAGE 90,
THE STAR IS ON PAGE 91, AND THE COW IS ON PAGE 92

COORDINATING ACCESSORIES

Ceramic kitchenware can be easily decorated to match or complement your colour scheme. Most commercial potteries sell undecorated seconds which can then be stamped with your own design. Continuing your kitchen style and colour scheme with coordinated accessories makes even a mass-produced kitchen look original and interesting.

The ceramics here have all been stamped using oven-bake ceramic paints which although non-toxic are not recommended to come into contact with food or your mouth. So the plates and mugs with an overall pattern are for decorative use only. However, by stamping simple borders and patterns around the outside of bowls, and by avoiding the rims of mugs, it is possible to decorate ceramics functionally as well.

With the exception of the daisy, each of the stamps shown opposite were made from a dense foam rubber following the technique described on page 13. The daisy, however, is a manufactured stamp – it is perfectly possible to use them on ceramics, but take care working around curved edges.

OPPOSITE: THE TEMPLATE FOR THE DAISY
IS ON PAGE 93

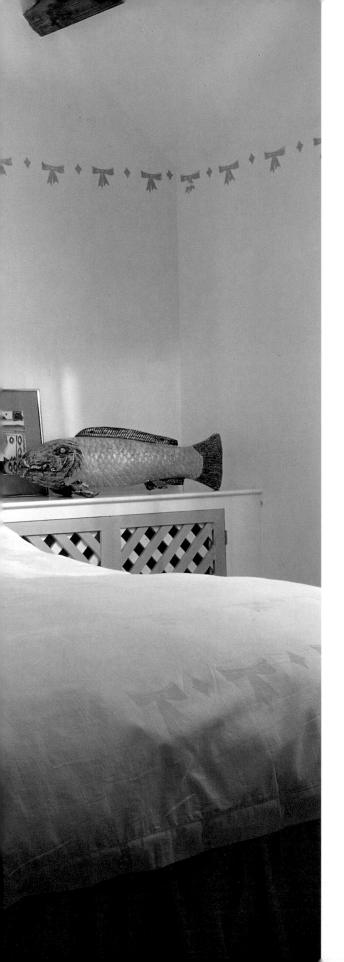

FIVE

Bedrooms

It is quite possible to change the colour scheme of a room without repainting all of it. For example, why not pick out an architectural feature, alcove or detail – such as the chimney breast shown here – and paint it a contrasting colour to the wall? The colour scheme can then be continued by painting your stamps and woodwork in the same colour.

To complement the blue trellis work and stamped bows – and also to add a little warmth and interest – the coronet above the bed featured to the left was painted a soft yellow to match the linen. But to avoid overdoing the bows, the coronet and all the bed linen was stamped with delicate diamonds (see overleaf). Further ideas for accessorizing your bedroom are given on pages 68-71 with hat boxes and decorative furniture.

UNIFYING MOTIFS

Bows alone can look somewhat prissy and flouncy, but when combined with a tiny diamond the effect becomes altogether different, evocative of the dainty ironwork found in the Caribbean. Likewise, muslin drapes evoke a sense of the exotic and as this fabric is very cheap, readily available and easy to stamp onto, it becomes the perfect material to hang from a coronet. Alternatively, you could tack it onto the ceiling, or hang it from a suspended pole, rather like an old linen hanger.

In order to prevent the decorative elements from becoming too diverse in this room, the blue paint has been maintained as the basic decorative colour. Blue stamped bows and trellis work are illustrated to the left, and the blue chimney breast is below. In this way, contrasting stamps can be used successfully to provide variation, and yet not a distraction.

While a yellow diamond has been used here, virtually any other design and colour would work equally well depending on the desired effect. Gold and silver look sumptuous, for example, and white on white looks positively dreamy and elegant.

ABOVE AND OPPOSITE:
THE TEMPLATES FOR THE DIAMOND AND THE BOW ARE ON PAGE 92

HAT BOXES

These pretty boxes are practical, decorative and very useful for adding a little something to a room. They are made from fine, recycled papier mâché and are sold unpainted, ready to be decorated at a whim (see suppliers on page 96). They obviously make ideal objects to stamp onto but you could also use any other box, even an old shoe box, perhaps cutting simple points in the lid to add delicate detailing.

The stripy box was painted using a stamp roller – an incredibly simple way to paint stripes. Working your way around the box, roll on stripes of one colour, allow to dry, and then fill in the gaps with rolls of another colour. The same technique could be applied horizontally. Use either emulsion or acrylic paint and stamp with the same paint or a stamp paint.

Lids of boxes such as these give scope for great originality. Of course, you can stamp them to match the main part of the box, but you could also choose to decorate them to contrast in a variety of ways. Choose different colours, different stamps, apply just one motif in the centre of the lid or go mad and stamp all over, perhaps leaving the main part of the box plain. The delicate gold border on the middle box, for example, is a fine detail and, again, was achieved with a stamp roller, this time being rotated gently along the scalloped edge with gold paint. If you intend using gold paint, it is worth choosing a good make to give a sense of preciousness. Stamp paint is especially effective. Inks could also be used although the effect might not be as strong and certainly gold ink will not leave the same lustre. Once fully stamped and dried, varnish the whole box with an acrylic varnish.

OPPOSITE: THE TEMPLATE FOR THE SHELL IS ON PAGE 90, THE STARFISH IS ON PAGE 91, AND THE BOW IS ON PAGE 92

SIMPLICITY

Being the most private room in the house, the bedroom is probably most likely to reflect the personality to the owner and is often a retreat from a hectic, family household. To this end, peaceful gold stars are extremely popular and look really beautiful on white. Alternatively, use dark cobalt blue to stamp with, or gold or silver on blue. If the ceiling is stamped all over it is probably just as well to leave the wall alone, although a simple border around a doorway or window looks incredibly effective through its sheer simplicity (see page 7). Understatement on the walls is especially necessary if you decide to stamp the furniture and bed linen as well. Some simple scatterings of the motif on a bedside table, such as that to the left for example, unifies a room's decor in a straightforward and charming way.

Unless you choose luxurious linen or Egyptian cotton, plain white bed linen is generally much cheaper than its patterned and coloured counterpart. If you cannot find plain white cotton bed linen it is very easy to make from white sheeting sold by the metre (yard) in most fabric shops. Make sure the sheeting is ironed and lay it flat on a floor to stamp.

ABOVE AND OPPOSITE:
THE TEMPLATE FOR THE STAR IS ON PAGE 92

SIX

Bathrooms

Bathrooms and toilets seem to be the most likely room in the house to be decorated in a more exuberant manner. Perhaps it is because they are generally the smallest rooms and therefore do not require such effort. They are certainly great starting points for a spot of stamping as you can let your imagination go wild, act on a whim, or simply create that special bathroom look that you have always craved. A small bathroom can be entirely changed in an evening, so why not put on some music, get out your stamps and paint and get going?

Virtually every method of interior stamping has been employed in this tiny and very jolly little bathroom. The walls, floors, tiles, furniture, blind and even the mirror have each been attacked with a combination of two simple stamps and some very bright paints. Obviously, if you find it all a bit too busy and prefer to live with a more reserved effect, you could leave the floor, tiles or bath panels plain white.

FLOORBOARDS AND CABINET

No surfaces have been spared in this bathroom. The pine floorboards were primed and then whitewashed with emulsion and once fully dried they were decorated with a manufactured stamp and stamp paint. As you can probably detect in the photograph, the floor was not marked out. Instead it was stamped by eye which is quite appropriate in this instance as the style is fun and casual. When the stamping was completed and paint dried, the whole floor was painted with two coats of matt polyurethane varnish.

The cabinet was first painted with a coat of maroon emulsion and left to dry. The Caribbean-style pink paint was then brushed on very roughly and sparsely with a dry paintbrush – it was not loaded with paint – left to dry and then stamped with two contrasting motifs. The walls were colour-washed using a basecoat of minty green and then a topcoat of a watered down mid-blue emulsion paint applied quickly with a paintbrush.

ABOVE AND OPPOSITE: THE TEMPLATE FOR THE STAR IS ON PAGE 92,
AND THE BLAZING STAR IS ON PAGE 93

BATHROOM ACCESSORIES

Gold and white always look sophisticated and rather luxuriant, and gold matches brass taps very well (or choose silver to match chrome). It is not difficult to find bathroom accessories embellished with gold, such as the tooth mug here, or you can decorate plain white ones yourself using gold ceramic paint, as shown on the tiles (see page 21). You could also stamp a plain soap dish and even the outside edge of the sink (too much swishing water will slowly wear away the stamps if put on the inside of the sink). The stamp on the tooth mug offers a contrast in pattern to the overall stamping in this particular bathroom, but you might prefer to use, say, a part of the main stamp or reduce it in size.

If you prefer, the abstract cross featured here could be successfully substituted with a more classic design such as a star or fleur de lys, or even with little golden fish.

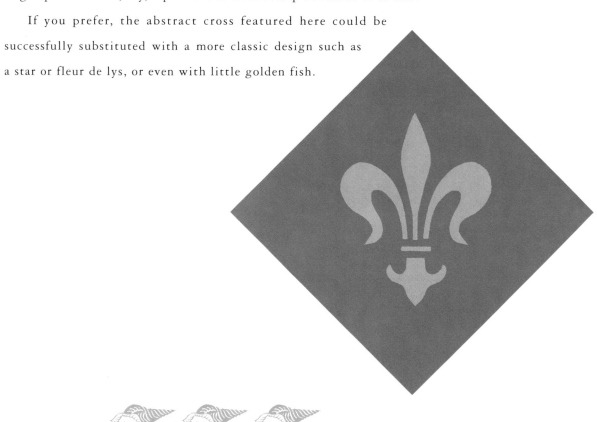

OPPOSITE: THE TEMPLATE FOR THE CROSS IS ON PAGE 95

BATHROOM LINEN

The seaside theme is probably the most popular of all bathroom decor and, indeed, any of the stamp designs on the previous pages could successfully be substituted with fish, shells, or boats to create that special beach hut look. Even the golden cross on the previous page could be replaced with tiny gold shells for a more refined shoreline.

These linen hand towels were bought from an auction which is often a good source of fine old linens, but you could make your own linen towels from old pillowcases, sheets or tablecloths. Linen bags and even bathrobes would also look very pretty stamped with little fish. Stamping onto ordinary fluffy towels is not recommended because of the rough texture of the material.

For some people, this grey-blue is a cool colour scheme, so perhaps add a dash of yellow, either in the form of another shell or a sun as shown to the left, to add some warmth. Of course, you needn't limit yourself to stamping the linen in your bathroom – cold ceramic paints are great for tiles (see page 21).

ABOVE AND OPPOSITE: THE TEMPLATE FOR THE SCALLOP IS ON PAGE 90, THE HEART IS ON PAGE 91, AND THE BOW IS ON PAGE 92

SEVEN

Nurseries

As stamping is so quick and inexpensive, it is the perfect method of decoration for children's rooms. In comparison with other rooms in the house, the decor needs changing more frequently to accompany growing children and you are far less likely to begrudge redecorating a nursery which only took a few hours to stamp in the first place and required no expensive designer fabrics.

These rather primitive animal designs are fun and appealing, and at the same time are also rather stylish. The white quilt cover and pillowcases have been randomly stamped with various elements of the same theme, and also in several different colourways (see page 71 for making ideas). Likewise, the curtains were made from cheap lining fabric and stamped to match the bed linen – but with an added border of mice to coordinate with the pelmet and border around the top of the room.

STRIPPED PINE FURNITURE

Stamping onto stripped pine furniture is both easy and very effective. The natural, soft tones of the wood provide a backdrop for a few jolly stamps to enliven children's furniture. This pretty chest of drawers was already lightly waxed and using stamp paints it was possible to stamp straight onto it. Paints like this are durable and so do not require varnishing.

The giraffe and tiger stamps have been given added interest by painting spots and stripes by hand and in a different colour. This same technique can be used with any stamps to create a two-toned print and would be especially useful if you were stamping a large area with a single design to add an extra dash of colour and shape. The chest of drawers could alternatively have been painted and stamped to match the chair. Or a similar effect could be achieved by substituting the animals with fruit and vegetables, numbers and letters, clowns, farm animals or even insects.

OPPOSITE: THE TEMPLATES FOR THE CROCODILE AND ZEBRA ARE ON PAGE 94, AND THE ELEPHANT IS ON PAGE 95

PAINTED FURNITURE

Having plain white walls leaves great scope for painted furniture which can be a great design solution to the various stages of growing up, allowing a scheme to be subtly changed with little effort. Furniture can be painted as often as you like, or as the child gets older can do it him- or herself. Unattractive pieces of furniture can be totally transformed with paint and stamps, even nasty old wardrobes found in skips. Stamping is then very easy as any mistakes can readily be wiped off with a damp cloth (see page 18).

The colours and designs on this box would suit a child from birth to teeny bopper. It was painted in a silk finished vinyl, left to dry and then stamped with stamp paints using some of the animals featured on pages 80-1 and the additional simple star to make a strong border. The lampshade was made from a kit (see page 47), covered in plain white paper and similarly stamped with two of the designs from the quilt and cover and curtains.

ABOVE AND OPPOSITE: THE TEMPLATE FOR THE PALM TREE IS ON PAGE 91, AND THE ELEPHANT IS ON PAGE 95

COT QUILT AND BUMPER

The theme in this nursery was designed to fit in with the room decor without matching it perfectly. The hearts complement the daisies on the wall and the multitude of colours are more appealing to a younger child. Nevertheless, the lifespan of baby decor is only about two years, and although there is certainly no need to alter the room in its entirety as the child moves from cot to bed, the cot linen will become redundant. For this reason it makes sense to make or cover your own cot quilt and bumper.

This pretty set was made from a cheap white cotton sheeting and stamped with multi-coloured, pastel hearts which suit either sex. Make long and well-attached ties for your cot bumper as it is important that it is securely fastened to a cot so that the child cannot remove it.

Once the cot linen has been designed, other pieces of furniture and accessories can be stamped to match to create a coordinated style. Curtains, toy boxes or trays which could be used to keep tidy all those baby creams, potions and lotions are particularly straightforward.

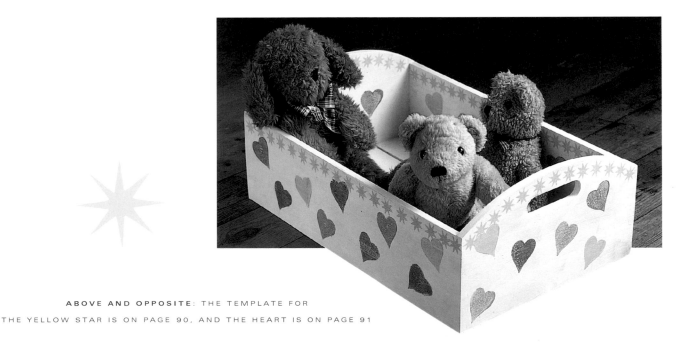

ABOVE AND OPPOSITE: THE TEMPLATE FOR THE YELLOW STAR IS ON PAGE 90, AND THE HEART IS ON PAGE 91

COORDINATED FURNISHINGS

This is, in fact, the same room as shown on the previous page, minus the cot, illustrating stage two of a child's bedroom. The bed, built from medium-density fibreboard, was designed to specifically fit into an alcove, so making good use of a little space.

The pretty daisy motif was stamped with a commercial stamp and stamp paint which can be used on both fabric and walls. The daisy would look equally good in yellow, pale blue or even a combination of colours. You could also paint over the daisy centre with another colour for added interest or stamp white daisies onto a coloured wall. Whichever combination you choose, daisies and pastel shades will always look pretty, fresh and feminine. For a boy's room, you could paint the bed blue and substitute pink daisies with blue sailing boats and fish.

To prevent the motif from becoming too repetitious, notice how the walls are stamped with a gridded pattern, the curtains with well spaced out rows, and the quilt with daisies that are much closer together.

OPPOSITE: THE TEMPLATE FOR THE DAISY IS ON PAGE 93

Templates

The outlines on these and the following pages are used throughout this book. To use them, either enlarge the motif of your choice on a photocopier to an appropriate size or use them directly from these pages. To transfer the outlines onto thin cardboard for use as a template, trace the motif onto tracing paper, or parchment paper, and then go over the back of the paper with a soft pencil. Position it on the cardboard and draw over the top of the outline once again.

1

2

3

1 star (*see pp.33, 34, 41, 60-1, 86*)
2 scallop (*see p.78*)
3 shell (*see p.69*)
4 heart (*see pp.26, 28, 38, 58, 60-1, 78, 86*)
5 star fish (*see p.69*)
6 palm tree (*see pp.49, 85*)
7 paisley (*see pp.47, 49*)

1

2

3

4

5

6

7

8

1   bow *(see pp.66, 69, 78)*
2   cow *(see pp.60-3)*
3   diamond *(see pp.67, 74-5)*
4   star *(see pp.45, 70-1)*
5   daisy *(see pp.28, 32, 58, 62, 89)*
6   grapes *(see p.53)*
7   blazing star *(see pp.74-5)*
8   holly leaf *(see p.34)*

1

2

3

4

5

6

7

8

9

1 crocodile *(see p.82)*
2 star *(see p.44)*
3 fish *(see p.54)*
4 crown *(see pp.45, 46)*
5 zebra *(see p.82)*
6 petals *(see p.29)*
7 elephant
   (see pp.82, 85)
8 fleur de lys *(see p.44)*
9 cross *(see p.77)*

SUPPLIERS

STAMPS

Blade Rubber Stamps
2 Neal's Yard, London WC2H 9DP
Tel: 0171 379 7391
(rubber stamps, ink pads, rollers and embossing equipment; mail order)

The English Stamp Company
Sunnydown, Worth Matravers, Dorset BH19 3JP
Tel: 01929 439117
Fax: 01929 439150
(all stamps featured in this book, stamp paint and rollers; mail order anywhere in the world)

Inca Stamp
136 Stanley Green Road, Poole,
Dorset BH15 3AH
Tel: 01202 660080
(rubber stamps, ink pads and embossing equipment; mail order)

John Lewis
Oxford Street, London W1
Tel: 0171 629 7711 for details of your nearest branch
(English Stamp Company stamps)

Paint Magic
116 Sheen Road, Richmond, Surrey SW9 1UR
Tel: 0181 940 5503
Fax: 0181 332 7503
(all decorating materials, including rubber and foam stamps; mail order)

PAINTS

C Brewer
327 Putney Bridge Road, London SW15 2PG
Tel: 0181 788 9335
(general painting suppliers with branches throughout Southern England)

Daler-Rowney Ltd
12 Percy Street, London W1A 2BP
(artist's materials)

Farrow & Ball Ltd
33 Uddens Trading Estate,
Wimborne, Dorset BH21 7NL
Tel: 01202 876141
Fax: 01202 873793
(National Trust Historical Paints; mail order)

Green & Stone
259 Kings Road, London SW3 5ER
Tel: 0171 352 0837
(artist's materials, including cold and oven-fired ceramic paints; mail order)

International Floor Paint
Tel: 01703 226722 for details of your nearest supplier
(suitable for tiles and available from most DIY shops)

The Stencil Store Company Ltd
91 Lower Sloane Street, London SW1W 8DA
Tel: 0171 703 0728
(cold ceramic paints; mail order)

MISCELLANEOUS

The Decorative Arts Company Ltd
5a Royal Crescent, London W11 4SL
Tel: 0171 371 4303
(paints and papier mâché blanks ready to decorate; mail order)

Habitat
Tottenham Court Road, London W1
Tel: 0171 631 3880 for details of your nearest branch
(plain cotton fabrics, plain crockery and wooden items)

Lampkits
16 Cliveden Road, London SW19 3RB
Tel: 0181 543 6255
(lampkits)

Limerick Linens
PO Box 20, Tanners Lane, Barkingside,
Ilford, Essex IG6 1QQ
Tel: 01268 284405
(inexpensive plain bedlinen and sheeting; mail order)

Ian Mankin
109 Regents Park Road, London NW1 8UR
Tel: 0171 722 0997
(linens and natural fabrics; mail order)

Paperchase
213 Tottenham Court Road, London W1P 9LD
Tel: 0171 580 8496
(papers; mail order)

Pentonville Rubber
48-52 Pentonville Road, London N1 9HF
Tel: 0171 837 0283

Provincial Rubber
105 Glenfrome Road, Bristol
Tel: 01272 541117

OVERSEAS SUPPLIERS OF THE ENGLISH STAMP COMPANY STAMPS

AUSTRALIA

Bloombury's of Melbourne
PO Box 2218, North Brighton, Victoria 3186
Tel: +61 3866 4321

BELGIUM

Tex-Artes
Kasteeldreef 10, 2950 Kapellen
Tel: +32 3664 3962
Fax: +32 3664 3841

A Priori
Vlasmarkt 32, 2000 Antwerp
Tel: +32 3266 3892
Fax: +32 3232 2259

GERMANY

Kirchner
Norderster Weg, 25899 Kleiseerkoog via Niebull
Tel: +49 4661 2233
Fax: +49 4661 2394

NETHERLANDS

Amazona
Van der Zaanlaan 9, 1215 SG Hilversum
Tel: +31 3523 7250
Fax: +31 3523 7250

SPAIN

Tons
Xiquets de Valls, 14 Esq Pl del Sol,
08012 Barcelona
Tel: 237 7820

USA

Contact **The English Stamp Company**
Tel: +44 1929 439117
Fax: +44 1929 439150